GALATIANS

THE LIFE I NOW LIVE

10 Publishing
a division of 10 of those.com

First published in Great Britain in 2015

British Library Cataloguing in Publication Data

A record for this book is available from the British Library

ISBN: 978-1-910587-09-6

Designed by Diane Bainbridge

Printed in the UK

10Publishing, a division of 10ofthose.com
9D Centurion Court, Farington, Leyland, PR25 3UQ, England
Email: info@10ofthose.com
Website: www.10ofthose.com

Peter Mead

36 UNDATED DEVOTIONS THROUGH THE BOOK OF GALATIANS

INTRODUCTION

When Paul returned from his first missionary journey, in about AD 49, he was distressed to hear that false teachers had been following him as he preached in southern Galatia. These false teachers were trying to undo the gospel impact of Paul's ministry. Paul was angry!

With a fire in his heart he wrote Galatians, his first epistle. The result is stunning. Galatians is a passionate defence of his own ministry and especially of the gospel. The letter to the Galatians can be described like C.S. Lewis' Aslan – it is neither safe nor tame, but it is so, so good. Why? Because it draws our hearts to the One who is good, to Christ, and to the wonder of living in fellowship with His Father, our good God.

Some might suggest Galatians is largely irrelevant today. After all, who would accept a preacher promoting circumcision, a key issue in Galatians? When Martin Luther wrote about Galatians he described both a black devil and a white devil. The first is all about sin as we tend to think of it – gross, immoral and hideous. The latter is when the enemy comes as an angel of light, couching his influence in very religious and apparently godly garb. For Luther, it was the white devil that was the greater threat to the gospel. The world at its best is really the world at its worst. We easily spot overt attacks on the gospel, but we are all susceptible when false teaching comes under the cover of godly religious instruction. The devil loves to corrupt our view of Christ and wreak havoc on our experience of the Christian life.

Paul was contending for the ongoing implications of the gospel for the Christian life. Luther wrote that, 'if we lose the doctrine of justification, we lose simply everything.'[1] The threat facing the young Galatian church is still alive and well today. Yet so is the glorious gospel Paul proclaimed. Luther also wrote, 'I know how often I suddenly lose sight of the rays of the Gospel and of grace, which have been obscured for me by thick, dark clouds.'[2] May our hearts be stirred as we study this powerful epistle together. May the rays of the gospel and of grace shine clearly in our hearts. And may our lives be transformed so that others will also be drawn to the wonderful gospel of God's glorious grace!

DAY 1

READ Galatians 1:1–5

Galatians launches with a bang! Paul's ministry and message have been attacked. Is he a true apostle? Is his message the true gospel? Is Paul's gospel too good to be true?

To begin, Paul could have simply written, 'Paul, to the churches in Galatia: grace and peace.' Since Paul wrote more than that, let's be sure to notice all that he added.

In verses 1–2 he defends his ministry. He is a true apostle. He was not sent by other men, or even a specific man (i.e. a key leader in Jerusalem). No, Jesus Christ and the Father commissioned him. Also, Paul is not a maverick minister, for there are brothers with him.

In verses 3–5 he presents the truth of the gospel that he had preached among them. Notice four important ingredients in the gospel mix here:

1. Sin is very serious. Everywhere we look, everything is shot through with evil. We are all sinners and we need to be rescued.
2. What rescues us from this present evil age? It is the grace of God our Father and Jesus Christ who gave Himself for our sins. Paul could have chosen to expand on this: He came to earth, went to the cross, died the death we deserved, and rescued us from sin. The gospel is about the gracious plan of God the Father and the Son working together to rescue sinners.
3. Notice in verse 5 that the grace of the Father and the Son working together results in all the glory going to God. The grace of God leads to the glory of God.
4. Look for our role in the rescue. Look carefully. What do you see? There is absolutely nothing about us! The gospel is God's grace at work. We don't earn it, deserve it, work at it, or add to it. In Paul's summary of the gospel we are simply recipients.

The gospel is all about the glorious grace of God that rescues sinners from evil. This was the message Paul preached in Galatia. His message transformed lives and established churches. Let's pray that this message also truly grips us!

REFLECTION

How much does the gospel you believe depend on the grace of God? How much does it depend on you?

DAY 2

READ Galatians 1:6–10

Galatians is a life-changer, but for many Christians it remains only a biblical curiosity – an ancient letter to a small region in central Turkey. Perhaps people think that the dangerous teaching Paul opposed back then poses no threat now. After all, if the problem was merely the promotion of circumcision, then we can relax. Believers with a Jewish background who were pushing circumcision would not get an invitation to most churches today.

Circumcision was certainly a feature of the false teaching, it was even used as the label for the false teaching, but the real issue was broader than just circumcision. It was an anti-gospel promotion of law-keeping.

This is what the false teachers were effectively saying, 'to be truly born again, not just born a bit, then you need the law, that is, to be circumcised. And if you want to live Christianity to the full, then you need to strive to keep the law. Paul's grace message needs balancing with law.'

Now at this point in a typical letter we would expect Paul to write, 'I give thanks to God for you ...' Not this time! Get ready for an explosion. Paul is indignant! Verse 6 is like a landmine waiting to go off if you poke around it for too long. 'I am astonished that you are so quickly deserting ...'

After hearing the gospel and responding to it, now the Galatians were turning away. They were not just turning away from a message, but were turning away from a person, from God Himself!

Here comes the explosion. How were they turning away from God? Were they diving into gross immorality? No. Were they leaving Christianity and signing up to some other religion? No. What were they doing? They were actually becoming *more* religious, *more* Jewish, and, they might say, '*more* biblical', even '*more* godly'!

Is it possible that a greater personal commitment to keeping the law could mean turning from God? That is what Paul is saying. How is that possible? Because any change and any addition to the gospel of God's grace in Christ Jesus is a different and distorted gospel. **Anything that takes our eyes off Christ and onto ourselves is really no gospel at all!**

Surely this can't be right? Either Paul is pro-sin, or he must have a better solution in mind.

REFLECTION

How could a greater commitment to so-called godliness actually be turning you from God? Do corruptions of the gospel stir appropriate anger in you?

DAY 3

READ Galatians 1:6–10

We live in an age where strong conviction is often discouraged. You can hold to what you believe as strongly as you like, but if you challenge what I believe, then I may label you an intolerant bigot. Somehow the idea that there might actually be true truth has gotten lost in the shuffle. Paul was clear on the importance of the truth, especially in respect to the gospel. **The gospel is worthy of indignant defence because it is all of God!**

Paul's meaning in verse 8 is, 'look, if I lost it and I came to you preaching a different message, or if an angel comes from heaven and preaches a different version of the gospel, (these things won't happen, but if they did): eternal condemnation – that's what I am calling for!' Paul was really strong in his conviction!

Verse 9 reinforces this statement. If anyone comes preaching a different message from the truth the Galatians received (which is exactly what was happening), then that person should be eternally condemned.

Some of us cannot help but want to neutralise any conviction we meet. 'Steady on, Paul, no need to be so strong!' we might argue. However, as far as Paul is concerned, if someone is trying to add law to God's grace, then eternal condemnation is what they deserve. He could not get any stronger!

The gospel is totally about God's grace. It has nothing to do with what we could do or will do. It is all about God's loving, self-giving grace. That's the gospel. Martin Luther wrote,

I personally would like to keep both the righteousness of grace as that which justifies and the righteousness of the Law as the basis for God's attitude toward me. But, as Paul says here, confusing these means perverting the Gospel of Christ.[3]

If you try to add law to the gospel, do you get more godliness? No, you actually get less. We will see that in chapter 5. If we add law and self-effort to the gospel, we will throttle the grace out of the gospel. In essence Paul is saying, 'No way! Don't go there! It will strangle; it will squash; it will kill.' How great must be the grace of God!

REFLECTION

If you were a Galatian, how would you feel to have an apostle fighting to protect you from false teaching? How important is the truth of the gospel for you?

DAY 4

READ Galatians 1:11–24

After the thanksgiving (but in this case, astonishment) section of an epistle, some biographical information would typically follow. Here Paul takes the opportunity to continue defending his ministry. As we look at Paul's life, let's celebrate a gospel-transformed life! In the next chapter he will return to the issue of his message.

At the same time, there is an important question to answer: is Paul's ministry trustworthy? This is important because thirteen books in our New Testament were written by him. If Paul got it wrong, or was imbalanced in his teaching, then we need to know. If Paul was a true apostle, then we can read his letters with confidence because they are God's word.

The false teachers who followed Paul around southern Galatia attacked his status as an apostle. They probably acknowledged that he was an apostle, but only a *deputy* apostle. The real apostles were the twelve in Jerusalem. Perhaps these had sent Paul out, but on the way to Turkey had he dropped half of their message out of his pocket?

In verses 11–17 Paul makes the source of his ministry clear. It was not from an apostolic seminar in Jerusalem, but by a revelation of Christ Himself. Paul had been a rising star in Judaism, a terrorist campaigning against the followers of Jesus. But God, by His grace, called Paul and revealed Jesus to him. He wanted to make Paul a preacher. Paul did not rush to Jerusalem, but to the desert of Arabia – he needed time to rethink everything he thought he knew!

Paul was called, not by men, but by God; he was trained not by men, but by God; he was sent not by men, but by God. Paul could be fully trusted as an apostle.

In verses 18–24 Paul continues his story. After three years he did pop up to Jerusalem for a visit and stayed a couple of weeks. He met only two apostles. After that he left the region. The believers in Jerusalem only heard rumours but to the effect: 'The terrorist is transformed and is now preaching the faith!'

The Judean churches were all of a twitter. God's grace had transformed Paul, and now God was being glorified. **Paul's ministry could be trusted because he was transformed: called, trained and sent by God.**

REFLECTION

What is the greatest gospel life-transformation story you know? Thank God for the transformation of Paul and the letters we have as a result!

DAY 5

READ Galatians 2:1–10

Paul was a true apostle, but what about his message? Was Paul's 'God's-grace-only' gospel enough, or did it need to be somehow balanced?

In these verses Paul tells of a later visit to Jerusalem, fourteen years after his conversion, to show that the apostles fully endorsed his message. Paul went with Barnabas and Titus to bring a love gift to the church (see Acts 11:27–30). The gift was a public display of unity, a Gentile gift for suffering Jewish-background believers.

Paul was not there to get his message endorsed by 'more senior' apostles. He was convinced his ministry was from God, but he did want to make sure they were all on the same page, that their public unity was supported by private reality. So privately Paul arranged a little conference.

Paul laid out his message. Did the apostles fix, add to, or balance it in any way? The answer eventually comes in verse 6. First, Paul tells of an incident involving Titus in verses 3–5. While he was there the very issue of circumcision came up because some false brothers infiltrated the ranks and kicked up a fuss about Gentile Titus. The false teachers were strongly resisted and Titus was not circumcised. What was the bottom line as far as the apostles were concerned? They were fully with Paul, so he could say 'they added nothing to my message' (v. 6).

In verses 7–10 Paul makes this agreement even clearer. The apostles not only added nothing to the gospel Paul preached but also recognised him on a level with Peter. The leading apostles did give Paul something. What did they give Paul? It was not a lecture, nor a correction. They gave him a hearty handshake as he headed out to the Gentiles, leaving them to focus on the local Jews. **Paul's message of God's grace was the gospel of all the apostles**.

When the apostles heard Paul's message about the grace of God, they were excited to stand with him in his ministry. In fact, they asked him for a favour – please don't forget the poor. For the rest of his career, Paul was always concerned to bring gifts from Gentile churches to Jerusalem to show unity because there is one gospel and one church. It is a church built upon the gospel of God's grace.

REFLECTION

How does the gospel of God's grace stir you to give to others in need? Does the gospel motivate you to care for the poor? And for church unity?

DAY 6

READ Galatians 2:11–14

In the previous section, Paul wrote about Peter and the apostles affirming his message. Now he takes it a step further and shows that once he had even corrected Peter. It all happened because of Jewish food laws.

The Old Testament had established what was clean and unclean, but Peter had received a vision from God to show that these laws no longer applied (see Acts 10:9–16). Nevertheless here Paul remembers a visit from Peter (Cephas) during which Peter changed back to law-keeping because of pressure from some folks coming from Jerusalem.

Peter's altered behaviour probably took place after the events of Acts 12, where we read of Herod wanting to kill Peter, whom he had imprisoned. Miraculously, Peter was released from prison. He headed to the coast and could easily have sailed north for a visit to Antioch.

Why are Paul and Peter in conflict? This was an era when Jewish nationalism was a growing movement. The gospel's message that Gentiles could come to God as Gentiles was not popular with the nationalists. So these visitors to Antioch applied pressure to Peter, Barnabas and others, who then returned to following Jewish dietary laws. Peter knew from his vision that he now had freedom to eat all kinds of food, but he started following the food laws anyway (vv. 12–13). Paul saw the division this caused in the mainly Gentile church at Antioch and stepped in to get the issue resolved. He opposed Peter to his face (vv. 11, 14)!

What was the reason for Paul's opposition to Peter? Because living the Christian life by trusting in your own law-keeping instead of keeping your eyes on Christ is inconsistent with the gospel. **The way we live as Christians must be in line with the truth of the gospel**.

By Acts 15 the controversy over the role of the law in salvation and the Christian life was fully resolved by a united church. There we read of Peter, Paul, Barnabas and James all being on the same page: Gentiles must not be expected to live like Jews to follow Jesus.

REFLECTION

What is there in your life, either good or bad, that is not in line with the truth of the gospel?

DAY 7

READ Galatians 2:15–21

After his stories of encounters with the other apostles, now Paul switches to the main argument of his letter. First, in verses 15–17, Paul shows that **justification before God is by faith and not by works**. Second, in verses 18–21, Paul shows that having been justified by faith, we also now live the Christian life by faith, united to Christ as we'll see in more detail on Day 8.

To be justified before God is an unspeakable privilege. It means to be declared right with God. It is the opposite of being condemned for our sin. Notice how many times Paul uses the word in verses 15–17. Even thoroughly Jewish apostles knew that trying to earn salvation by keeping the law is not how it works. Salvation, whatever your background, whatever your level of personal morality, is only possible by trusting Jesus Christ. (Remember that faith, belief and trust are all words for the same idea.)

In verse 15 Paul refers to the Gentiles with this typically Jewish label – 'Gentile sinners' (ESV). This is because the Gentiles had no regard for the law. By verse 17 Paul recognises that Jewish followers of Jesus could also be labelled as sinners because they weren't passionate about the law. So does this faith-gospel that seems light on law make Jesus a promoter of sin? Paul replies to this accusation in the strongest possible terms: 'Absolutely not!'

We all struggle to shake an assumption ingrained in our fallen world – specifically, that righteous living is something we can achieve by our effort to keep rules. So even though the gospel declares that we can only be justified by faith, not by works of the law, still we will find ourselves continually pulled back to our ingrained assumption that we need to try hard to be good.

It is so easy to confuse the gospel message with language of personal commitment and renewed moral effort. Paul will definitely explain how God will make us holy, but let us be really careful to never let our understanding of justification be diluted, or even poisoned, by mixing in our own effort to the gospel of grace.

REFLECTION

Being good does not make anyone acceptable to God – how would you explain this to a friend? If you have trusted in Christ and His death, you will not be condemned by God – do you really believe this to be true?

DAY 8

READ Galatians 2:15–21

Just as our justification comes by faith, not by law-keeping, so once we are saved, we do not turn back to the law. **There is a whole new way of living this new life, and it comes from being united to Christ in His death and His life.**

Living a life of moral effort does not justify anyone. With respect to the law, Paul could have said, 'I learned. I tried. I failed.' The law had shown him to be a failed sinner, so he stopped trying to find life that way. Instead of looking to the law, that is to himself, Paul had discovered what it meant to live for God (v. 19).

In verse 20 Paul explains the key feature of this new way of living. As he looks to Christ instead of to his own efforts, he so identifies himself with Christ that he sees himself as co-crucified, and also now co-living with Him.

To ponder Christ dying for us is staggering, but Paul goes further. He saw himself as so united to Christ that when Christ died, Paul died. Is that a strange thought? Actually, what a relief it is! After all our striving and failure, that futile self-effort life is finished: it is dead with Jesus.

More than that, when we think about the living Christ, we are thinking about the new life which is ours! Jesus did not just rise from the dead to give us life after we die. Jesus lives and wants to give us life now!

How can we still be in the same body, yet have a whole new life? By faith: as we fix the gaze of our hearts on Christ, looking intently at Him, instead of looking at ourselves and our efforts, we discover His life is now our life.

When this new life grips us, verse 21 brings us full circle to the thought of verse 16. Why would we want to set aside God's grace and waste our time trying to be good enough in our own strength? It never worked before, and turning back to ourselves would make Christ's death pointless.

REFLECTION

Which do you prefer: to look at yourself and your continual failure to live up to your own standards? Or to look at Christ, who loved you and gave Himself for you? Your flesh will pull you toward the first option, but there should be no contest: He is better by far!

DAY 9

READ Galatians 3:1–6

We 'get on' the same way we 'got in' – by faith. We don't get saved by our efforts and we don't grow by our efforts. But the false teachers had cast a spell on the Galatians and Paul is ready to startle the young Christians into realising it.

In the first verse Paul describes his own ministry among them. He had not focused his teaching on what they must do: top tips for living the Christian life or personal coaching in personal spirituality. His ministry in their midst was simple: he preached Christ and Him crucified (see also 1 Cor. 2:1–5). It was as if he had painted a huge billboard-sized poster of Christ crucified: a big, bold, vivid, striking portrait of Calvary.

In verse 2 Paul asks whether they were saved, and therefore received the Holy Spirit, by their effort to keep the law, or by responding to his message with faith. It had been the latter.

So in verse 3 we see the thought restated for greater impact: if you started by faith, that is, by the Spirit, do you now think that you will progress to maturity by works of the law, that is, by the efforts of your flesh? Paul calls this common approach to Christian growth foolish.

Paul is so perplexed that they would turn their backs on the gospel so easily that he follows up with more questions. First, in verse 4, he asks if the suffering that came with their faith in Christ was really pointless since they have now turned away from the gospel? Second, in verse 5, does the ongoing work of God by His Spirit really occur due to their efforts, or by means of their faith?

The gospel works by faith. It saves people as they believe. It grows people as they believe. In fact, Paul is so astonished by their turn from the gospel, he even points out that it has always worked this way: Abraham 'believed God, and it was credited to him as righteousness' (v. 6, quoting Gen. 15:6). He will develop the Abraham example in the following verses, but let's not move too quickly past the strong start to chapter 3.

REFLECTION

In what ways might Paul be upset with you for starting the Christian life by faith, but then striving to grow as a Christian by your own efforts?

DAY 10

READ Galatians 3:6–9

Paul referred to the Spirit three times in the first five verses of chapter 3. It is by the Holy Spirit that Christ lives in us and we are united to Him. It is not the law that gives us righteousness; it is the Holy Spirit of God at work in us. The law shows us where we are falling short, but it does not make us holy. What is it that produces righteousness in us? The life and love of God, given by the Spirit.

At this point it would make sense for Paul to launch into an overt presentation of all that is new in Christianity, with the Holy Spirit as the key feature of this New Covenant faith. After all, he wants the believers in Galatia to fully live the new life offered in Christ. Indeed, he will present the elements of the New Covenant in these next chapters, and he will focus on the Spirit. However, rather than presenting the 'newer and better' faith, Paul makes a move of strategic genius here – he goes 'old school'.

The Galatians were probably captivated by the false teachers, in part, because of how Jewish their teaching sounded. It was old, it sounded biblical and they thought, therefore, it was right. So Paul does not just go for a newer and shinier version of faith in God. He goes deliberately for an older one! He goes back before Moses all the way to Abraham. **God's plan has always been to draw people to Himself by faith rather than performance.**

Paul wants the Galatians to be immersed in Scripture as he reminds them of how the gospel works. In verse 6 he goes back to the key moment when Abraham believed God and therefore was counted as righteous. Then in verses 7–9 Paul shows that it is faith-folks, not law-keepers, who are truly sons of Abraham. Indeed, even Gentiles being saved apart from the law was anticipated in God's great promise to Abraham (see Gen. 12:1–3). Salvation has always been about faith, not law-keeping.

REFLECTION

Think about an area of your life where you struggle with sin – what can you do, in respect to that struggle, to shift your focus from yourself and your efforts to be holy, onto God and all that He has done for you?

DAY 11

READ Galatians 3:10–14

Back at the beginning of the chapter, Paul made several references to the Holy Spirit. Then he showed that true children of Abraham will always be those who believe, who put their faith in God, rather than those who obsess over law-keeping.

In verses 10–13 Paul continues to contrast relying on works of the law and faith in Christ. On the one hand, in verse 10, everyone who tries to keep the law and fails in even one detail is cursed – here Paul quotes Deuteronomy 27:26. By contrast, in verse 11, he quotes Habakkuk 2:4 to show that the righteous person lives by faith.

Back to the law again, in verse 12 Paul shows that it cannot be merged or blended with faith. We either live by law or by faith. Yet by faith in Christ, as Paul shows in verse 13, Christ bought us back from the curse of the law by becoming a curse for us as He hung on the tree at Calvary (this time quoting Deut. 21:23).

When we arrive at verse 14, we are back to the blessing of Abraham for the Gentiles. This was mentioned in passing in verse 8, but now we have an added detail. The blessing promised to believing Gentiles is the promise of the Holy Spirit!

Why is the Holy Spirit the promised blessing? Because the loss of the Spirit was at the centre of the fall of humanity right back at the beginning. When Adam and Eve sinned, they began to die physically, but they instantly died spiritually. That is, the Spirit who had united them in fellowship with each other and God was gone and they curved in on themselves. But God promised to solve the sin problem and here is the resolution – Christ's death at Calvary has bought the Spirit for believers! We can now be united with Christ again.

Paul is not contrasting determined law-keeping effort with a simple mechanism of faith. **The key to salvation and the Christian life is not mere faith; it is the presence of the Holy Spirit Himself!**

REFLECTION

How important is the Holy Spirit to your understanding of the gospel and living the Christian life? In what ways does the Holy Spirit direct your heart to Christ?

DAY 12

READ Galatians 3:15–18

Paul really wants the Galatians to be clear that God's promise and their performance are not to be blended in their understanding of the Christian life. In these verses he shows that God established a covenant with Abraham long before the law was added. More than that, adding the law did not change the nature of that covenant.

Verse 15 establishes the principle: a covenant, once established, is not changed by other circumstances. If I write a will leaving my personal library to a specific family member, and then someone gives me a box of books, that doesn't change the will.

Specifically in reference to Abraham, in verse 16, Paul states that God made promises to him and to his seed. Paul makes the point that while the term 'seed' or 'offspring' can be a collective plural (i.e. lots of them), the ultimate fulfilment would be a singular seed or offspring – specifically Jesus Christ, the promised seed of the woman (Gen. 3:15) and the promised seed of Abraham (Gen. 12:7; 13:15; 15:18; 24:7).

With the principle of the unchangeable covenant-promise established, Paul goes on to show in the next two verses (vv. 17–18) that the law does not change God's plan. The covenant had been ratified by God. In Genesis 15:8–21 Abram wanted to know how he could trust God's stated plan. He was told to fetch a collection of specific animals, which he then cut in two and arranged for a covenant ceremony. The significance of the ceremony is: if I don't fulfil my part of this agreement, may this killing and cutting be done to me!

Typically the two parties would walk together through the gruesome display of death, thus committing themselves to the agreement in the most solemn way possible. What happened in Genesis 15? Abram slept and God made the covenant Himself. Was God's promise to Abraham dependent on Abraham's performance? Not at all; it was to be blessing based on promise, not blessing based on performance.

The giving of the law did not change God's plan to give the blessing of salvation based on promise, not performance. On day 13 we will ask the obvious question: why give the law at all?

REFLECTION

How does it encourage your heart to know that your salvation is based on God's promise, not your own performance?

DAY 13

READ Galatians 3:19–22

Walking through Galatians should stir a very appropriate question in your heart: why did God give the law? If the law didn't change God's plan to save and bless people based on His promise, why did God give it at all? Surely the law was given either to help us get saved or to help us grow once we are saved? Paul does not see it that way.

Here Paul gives both a reason and a time frame for the law. The law was given because of sin, and the law was given 'until' the promised Seed should come (v. 19).

The reason the law was given was to highlight failure. As you read through Exodus and Leviticus you can observe a progression of the failure of God's people, followed by the giving of God's law, followed by further failure, and then more law. In 1 Timothy 1:8–11 Paul writes that there is a right way to use the law, and that is to identify sin. It is for the ungodly and sinners, not for the just.

As we read through the Bible, the law shines a light on our failure to love God and live for Him. Does this contradict the promises of God to bless us through the coming promised Seed? Not at all, for the law was never intended to produce righteousness (v. 21). The law doesn't contradict the gospel. It is just that the law is not the gospel.

The time frame for the law becomes the focus in verse 22. Here Paul introduces the language of imprisonment, of being locked up. **The law imprisons everything under sin so that we know we are trapped and need a rescuer**. The law was given to prepare a sinful world for the coming of Christ: the Rescuer of those who believe and trust in Him. Those who weren't looking for Jesus were imprisoned under sin. Humanity was in real trouble and needed to know it.

REFLECTION

How convinced are you of your absolute hopelessness apart from Christ? For a few moments ponder what you know of God's law and how it shows you your sin, then turn your gaze back onto Christ and express your praise for the gospel!

DAY 14

READ Galatians 3:23–29

Last time, we saw how humanity was imprisoned under the law, hopelessly unable to find relationship with a holy God. Everyone was held captive under the law until faith in the promised Seed could be revealed.

Paul then adds another image to reinforce the same point. We were also under the guardianship of a tutor – the law – for the same purpose. The guardian would raise a child during the immature years of life, but 'in Christ Jesus' we are now grown 'children of God through faith' (v. 26). Instead of being under external compulsion (a tutor), we are baptised into Christ and have put on Christ (v. 27 ESV). We no longer need to live under the guardian, because now we have Christ (vv. 24–25).

How can we be immersed in Christ and be 'wearing' Christ? This is another place where Paul is thinking of the Holy Spirit. We are baptised into Christ by the Spirit, which means that we are united to Him and have Him living in us (remember 2:20: 'I have been crucified with Christ and I no longer live, but Christ lives in me. The life I now live in the body, I live by faith in the Son of God'). At the same time, by the Spirit's work in our lives, the character of Christ becomes our character. Paul will develop this further in chapter 5.

One last thought before we leave the chapter. Since the gospel is not about what we bring to God, this means that Christianity is a truly inclusive faith. The result of salvation is that we are not differentiated based on nationality, status, or gender ... we are all equally lost, and we can all be equally saved as we simply trust in Christ (vv. 28–29).

We live in a culture that panics at the thought of anyone being excluded from anything. Often Christianity is the target of criticism because Christianity claims that Jesus is the exclusive way to come into relationship with God. Yet only Christianity is a truly inclusive faith! Whoever we are, irrespective of what we have done, or our nationality, or our social status, or our gender ... **whoever we are, by faith we can be heirs of God's great promise in the person of Jesus Christ**.

REFLECTION

Where do you find your own heart straying into illegitimate prejudice toward others? Is it race, colour, class, gender?

DAY 15 — **READ** Galatians 4:1–7

In Paul's day only a son could be an heir. That is why Paul uses here the language of 'sons' rather than 'children' as he writes this section. But this is not restricting salvation to men only. As he stated at the end of chapter 3, salvation is open to either gender. Paul is just making sure the Galatians see the full richness of the salvation promise. The offer is not just to be a child of God, but a child with all the rights of an heir!

The chapter begins, though, by stating that the heir is functionally no different from a slave as long as he is a child in training (vv. 1–2). However, once the date of maturity arrives, everything changes. The same is true for us! There was a time in God's plan when His people were imprisoned, enslaved and under guard (v. 3). The law was the guardian. We were caught in the operating system of this world: that is, the notion that we can live by our own self-directed obedience to external rules. (Paul refers to the same thing in Colossians 2:20–23.)

Then in verses 4–5 we read of the rescue! The rescue came at just the right time in God's plan. Even better than the timing though, is the identity of the Rescuer: God sent His own Son to rescue us. He became one of us, being born of a woman. Paul is referring to the wonder of the incarnation – that God's Son would actually become fully human in order to rescue us. Not only did He become fully human (while remaining fully God), He also entered our prison by being born under the law.

Once the Son of God had come all the way to us, He paid the full price to redeem us so that we could go all the way back to the Father with Him! **We are not just rescued slaves: we are rescued to be sons of the perfect Father with Jesus.**

REFLECTION

Does your life give off the vibe of being an imprisoned slave striving to be good, or the joyous freedom of being a child of the most wonderful Father?

DAY 16

READ Galatians 4:1–7

Paul packs such a punch into these few verses. He writes of our enslavement to a world system that demands performance from us, but then immediately writes of God's great rescue plan. It was perfectly timed and it involved the most perfect Rescuer: God's very own Son. Jesus came all the way from the embrace of His Father in heaven to the prison of life under the law. And then He paid the price to buy our freedom.

What is the language Paul uses to refer to our freedom? It is adoption and sonship. Think about it, a child is restricted by rules and training for adulthood, but a grown son has all the freedom and benefits you can imagine. He has the delight of intimate relationship with the Father, as well as all the benefits that come from being a full heir of everything the Father has.

Jesus' rescue does not simply buy us a set of benefits, such as an eternal entry ticket to heaven. Jesus buys us the most valuable gift of all: the Spirit of the Son Himself. We may live in a world of independence and interpersonal distance, but that is not God's design. The Father and the Son have forever delighted in profound intimacy by the Spirit. And that Spirit is now given to us so that our hearts ring with the delightful cry of 'Abba!', that is, 'Daddy!' (v. 6).

Think about it this way: Jesus gave everything to rescue people proven by the law to be sinners. We did not deserve anything, but He rescued us. He gave everything to get to us. He gave everything to rescue us. And amazingly, He gave us everything in that rescue. What do I mean? Well, we were not simply set free from the prison to live on the outside somewhere. **Jesus came to rescue us and bring us into the full fellowship of His family**. Now His Abba is our Abba! The fellowship of the Trinity is the fellowship that is ours!

This is an amazing truth. Perhaps you might like to look at Romans 8, especially verses 12–17, for more of the same!

REFLECTION

Imagine the best possible relationship with the best possible Abba, and then ask God to lead you into that privilege which is already yours in Christ!

DAY 17

READ Galatians 4:8–11

The good news of Christianity is that we can know and be known by God. The God of the cosmos who created everything actually cares to know about you and me. He knows your name. Actually He knows much more than that, because the very idea of 'being known' goes so far beyond simply knowing about a person. To know God is more than knowing facts about Him, and to be known by God is more than simply being registered in the files of His all-knowingness.

When the Bible talks about a person knowing a person, there is a profound sense of intimacy and connection involved. It is a person-to-person, heart-to-heart, deep connection kind of knowing.

But the Galatians were losing their grip on the wonder of being known by God. So Paul reminds them that before they knew God, they were living lives enslaved by non-gods (v. 8) – perhaps idols they worshipped. They had been trapped and stuck, but then they heard the gospel and responded. Now, bizarrely, they were choosing to go back to being slaves of non-gods (vv. 9–10).

Is Paul saying here that they were turning from God back to idolatry? Not at all. Their turn now is back to a godless pseudo-Christianity, rather than godless irreligion. There may be differences, but the underlying theme is the same. When we follow the elementary principles of this world we are striving to please some system or some expectation, rather than living for the pleasure of God.

So the Galatians were not rejoining the pagan temples. They were pursuing a legalistic godliness (v. 10). But their turn was away from the life-changing privilege of being known by God. Instead of living in relationship with God, they were turning to self-driven religiousness. This is more dangerous than overt idol worship, since the participant thinks they are being more godly.

This would be like the younger son in Luke 15 coming back into relationship with his dad, and then promptly choosing to head outside and become a 'religious' person like his older brother. Remember that without relationship with their Abba, both boys wanted dad's benefits while not wanting him, and both brought shame on him. **Too many followers of Jesus are drawn away from the gospel, not by worldly immorality, but by worldly religiosity.**

REFLECTION

What aspects of a legalistic religiosity attract you?

DAY 18

READ Galatians 4:12–20

In this section Paul wants to contrast two types of Christian ministry. He contrasts his own gospel work with the law-heavy shepherding of the other group. He wants the Galatians to play 'spot the difference'. **There are two types of ministry and the two types of fruit are starkly different**.

When Paul went to Galatia, he became like the people there (v. 12). He appropriately conformed his life to theirs so that he could win them with the gospel (see also 1 Cor. 9:19–23). In fact, Paul apparently stopped in Galatia because of some illness that curtailed his travel plans. In his weakness he boldly gave himself away as he preached the gospel to them (v. 13). His difficulty was a real gift to them, though, because he brought the message of Christ Jesus. Their response? They were filled with joy and ready to give of themselves for him, if only they could (v. 15).

Love and joy are the first two descriptions in the list of the fruits of the Spirit (mentioned in the next chapter). The gospel of Christ Jesus transformed lives in Galatia! But now Paul is perplexed (v. 20). The Galatians have traded in the wonder of the gospel for the liabilities of the alternative law-based system of godliness. Now when Paul communicates the truth to them, they treat him as an enemy (v. 16).

The men who were teaching a different gospel had a very different ministry profile. They were flattering the Galatians, but only so that the Galatians would make a big deal of them (v. 17). Paul longed to be with the Galatians again so that he could speak with a tender tone. Paul was not driven by a need for the Galatians to 'like him', but he called for them to 'become like him'. More than that, his great goal was for Christ to be formed in them (v. 19).

The false teachers wanted to be liked, to get a loyal following, to control the people. When the law is used to shepherd a church, we will always see behaviour police patrolling the pews. When the law reigns over a group of God's people, self-giving love will fade away, joy will evaporate and devotion to God as Abba will shift into a colder variation.

REFLECTION

Which type of ministry do you see in the church today? Which type do you see in your own heart, and practise?

DAY 19

READ Galatians 4:21–31

Paul is coming to the end of his main argument against the non-gospel promotion of law for Christian living. In the next chapter he will summarise what he has written and then go on to discuss the difference the gospel makes in daily life. But first, he finishes this section with a flourish. He tells a story. He paints a picture. And this picture is in black and white. Again, the contrast is huge.

Paul uses the story of Abraham to write figuratively in an allegory. Looking back to Genesis 12–22, Paul paints innocent slave Hagar in negative hues and complicit, disbelieving wife Sarah in positive. While that seems unfair, his goal is to give a biblical picture of the situation: **there are two versions of Christianity and they cannot live together**.

The false teachers loved to associate themselves with Jerusalem as supposed children of Abraham. So Paul offers a two-sided picture of the situation in Abraham terms. He paints the two sons of Abraham as the fruit of two versions of gospel ministry. One, Ishmael, is born by fleshly human effort that tries to help God work out His righteous plans, and this side of the story is characterised by slavery (vv. 23a, 24–25). The other son, Isaac, is born by faith in God's promise, according to the Spirit, and is characterised by freedom (vv. 23b, 26).

There were two different sons, but these two could not co-exist in the same family (v. 29). Likewise Paul resists any idea of blending his gospel with the false message that had been preached since his departure (vv. 30–31). Paul also says there are two different Jerusalems: one is the law-gripped earthly one, the other is the heavenly one to come.

Paul's allegory offers a positive encouragement: there is hope for the spiritually barren who will trust in God's promise (v. 27). But there is also an implicit warning: there will also be persecution. The law-obsessed folks will always persecute the grace-gripped free folks. A faith characterised by trust in God's grace will always be threatening to a self-reliant perversion of the real thing. Seeking to co-exist will ultimately fail. So Paul urges the Galatians to get rid of the law-enslaved brigade lest they corrupt the true church.

REFLECTION

Have you, like Abraham, ever relied on yourself to do God's work? Does your Christianity fit the Isaac profile, or the Ishmael profile?

DAY 20

READ Galatians 5:1

Paul now goes on to summarise his argument before shifting the focus back onto the Galatians in order to make some applications to them.

This verse is like a rallying cry to finish chapters 3–4: the gospel is all about setting sinners free! But that freedom is under threat. People will try to swamp it, throttle it and undo the freedom that is found in Christ. Paul wants the Galatians to resist that and remain free.

At its core, the false teachers' critique of his message was that Paul was soft on sin. Galatians is not a debate about whether Christians should sin or not. Paul is not saying we are free from the law so that we can sin freely (see v. 13). But God has provided a better solution for sin than the Old Covenant. Paul is arguing that the law was never intended to be a solution for sin. **The law highlights the sin problem, but it doesn't solve it**.

Paul took sin far more seriously than the serious-faced legalists did. Why? Because he knew that sin comes from within, so it is a much deeper problem than just behaviour. Therefore, God's solution has to address the very heart of the human problem, which is the human heart. Any solution that does not address the heart does not truly deal with sin.

The law in the Old Covenant was like a rumble strip beside the motorway. It made it clear when you were drifting off the road. The rumble strip helps the driver avoid disaster, but it does not make them a good driver.

A mirror, like the law, shows you when something is not right. But the mirror does not fix the problem. You do not take the mirror off the wall and scrub your face with it. The mirror is a good thing, but the mirror does not solve the problem.

The law serves a purpose, but it does not solve the problem because the law cannot create righteousness in anyone. But the gospel does make us righteous and compels us toward goodness – God has done that in Christ. So we must not slide back into a reliance on the law, for that would mean turning our backs on Christ and on the gospel.

REFLECTION

When you focus on keeping rules, is your gaze on Christ or on yourself?

DAY 21

READ Galatians 5:1–4

Paul wanted to stir the Galatians with his rallying cry of freedom in Christ (v. 1). Now he follows up with a warning to explain why a shift toward law-keeping is so dangerous (vv. 2–4). 'Mark my words!' is like writing 'Don't miss this!' – he wants their attention at this key point in his letter.

Why must they stand firm against this law teaching? Because if they choose to accept circumcision as the entry point into a supposedly righteous and godly lifestyle, then there are two consequences that automatically follow. First, Christ is of no value to them (v. 2). Second, they would be obligated to obey the whole law (v. 3).

Christ is such a complete Saviour. He is God's beloved Son and the promised deliverer who was born under law to pay the price and set us free. He is the one who loved us and gave Himself for us, who became a curse for us. He is the way that we can now receive the promised Spirit so that from our hearts we cry 'Abba!' to the Father as sons alongside the Son. Because of Jesus we can have fellowship with the Trinity, which is to truly live!

The alternative is to remain in the false life of self-focused effort and performance. As far as Paul is concerned, the gospel declares a divine 'No!' to anything less than a 100 per cent Jesus gospel. **The moment we add any element of law-keeping to our salvation package, we lose Jesus**. He is a complete Saviour and we cannot make Him play the part of partial saviour.

Furthermore, not only is Christ all or nothing, so too is the law all or nothing. The Bible does not divide the law into different categories. Paul is clear – put yourself under a bit of the law and you have to keep it all!

In verse 4 Paul is not opening up a debate about whether we can lose our salvation or not. He is trying to shock the Galatians and wake them up. He wants them to see that they cannot live in the gospel and then add the law back in. They should stick with what God has given them in Christ.

REFLECTION

What is your default 'Christ : self' ratio when you think about your salvation and living the Christian life? Does 100% : 0% feel uncomfortable? Why?

DAY 22

READ Galatians 5:5–6

Paul does not simply warn the Galatians about the danger of trying to add law-keeping to the gospel. He also offers the positive side of his argument again in verses 5–6.

The glorious gospel is truly good news: we have so much in Christ that we do not need to add in law-keeping. **Faith in Christ really is enough!**

Notice four aspects of his gospel summary in these two verses:

1. The gospel is by faith. This is in contrast to works. Paul does not mean that faith is therefore passive, because true faith does work. By the end of verse 6 he makes clear the importance of faith working itself out through love.
2. This gospel faith is in Christ, who is 'the hope of righteousness' (v. 5, ESV). The true believer trusts in Christ; they do not trust in themselves. This means that neither religious moralism (circumcision) nor irreligious licentiousness (uncircumcision) can generate what the gospel does through faith in Christ.
3. Gospel faith is not just concerned with the entry point into this new life. It is an ongoing reality: we eagerly wait for Him and our faith continues to work through love.
4. The ongoing gospel life is lived out 'through the Spirit' (v. 5), who is the key to the Christian life. As Paul goes on in his letter, he is going to focus in on God's amazing provision of the Holy Spirit. Sneak a quick look ahead to 5:16: living in step with the Holy Spirit is the counterpoint to living a sinful life!

The Christian life begins by faith and continues by faith – faith in the promised Christ. And the Spirit of Christ brings that ongoing intimacy with Christ, stirring us to eagerly wait for Christ, and to love others as the outworking of our faith in Christ. Paul's language here is vivid and striking. He is convinced God has truly provided a solution to our deepest problem.

REFLECTION

In what ways does the Spirit stir you to love Christ and others?

DAY 23

READ Jeremiah 31:31–34

Before we continue into the last section of Galatians, let's take a step back for a moment. The themes that Paul has written about so far are New Covenant themes. What is the New Covenant? Back in the prophets of the Old Testament, we read about this future New Covenant. The nation was under the law, but was this producing righteousness? No. The Law and the Prophets were merely showing them how desperately sinful they were.

So in passages like Ezekiel 36, Jeremiah 31 and Isaiah 40–66 God promised a New Covenant, one that would actually answer the sin question and not just highlight the problem. Here are three big features of this promise:

1. Sins are forgiven – God promised to release sinners from the guilt of their sin.
2. New hearts are fashioned – God promised to replace hearts of stone (dead hearts) with living hearts and to write the law on these new hearts so that His people would actually want to live righteously.
3. An intimate relationship begins – God promised to give His Spirit to His people and to bring them into a close relationship with Him.

Do we see these features in the argument of Galatians? Absolutely! Why would we turn from such good news back to the old external code of righteousness?

The New Covenant is God's plan to turn sinners into lovers of a loving God! So as we look at the summary of the main argument in 5:1–6, we see Paul re-introduces the term, 'love' in his description of the Christian life (v. 6). Both Christ and the Spirit have a critical role in stirring our love for God and others.

Back in 2:20 Paul wrote of Christ 'who loved me and gave himself for me'. It is like two bookends around the body of the letter. Paul is saying Christ loved me, I trust Him, and now that trust generates love in me too.

You cannot legislate for love. National governments cannot enact laws requiring people to love. It cannot be forced, because love is always a response. John put it this way, 'We love because he [God] first loved us' (1 Jn. 4:19). Our faith in Christ generates a New Covenant kind of response – from the inside out, so we have a heartfelt love that could never be achieved by an externally imposed code of conduct.

REFLECTION

How much does Christ's love for you stir you to respond in love?

DAY 24

READ Galatians 5:7–12

The main argument of Galatians has been presented. Having summarised it, now in these verses Paul warns the Galatians once more before he shifts onto the important question: why does all this matter? This warning is very strong: **balancing truth with error never improves the truth!**

In verses 7–8 he uses a running analogy to ask who has cut in on them to keep them from obeying the truth of the gospel. He knows the answer, but wants them to realise the impact the false teachers have had on their faith. They were following Christ, but now they have been persuaded in a different direction. Just like in 1:6, Paul wants them to know that they have turned away from God in their pursuit of a supposedly greater godliness.

In verse 9 he quotes a proverb about a little yeast being so pervasive. Why? Because he knows human nature. He knows that they have reacted to the false teachers and will soon react to his letter as well. They will probably pursue some sort of balance between the two extremes: a bit of grace and a bit of legalism; a bit of God at work and a bit of me at work. Balance is always good, isn't it? Not always. Balance can be exactly the wrong thing to pursue. A little bit of yeast affects the whole batch of dough. A little bit of error will destroy the truth. After all, it makes no sense to add a bit of poison to healthy vegetables in pursuit of a balanced diet.

In verse 10 Paul's confidence speaks through. He is miles away and they have manipulative and persuasive false teachers with them, but Paul does not panic. Here Paul practises exactly what he preaches – confidence in the Lord. God changes hearts, softens hearts, and brings people around to the truth. God can lead the hardest person to repentance. Paul knew this because he had been that person! He knew God could convince them of the truth of the gospel, and he knew God would bring consequences to those who were twisting the gospel. Paul's confidence in God offers a powerful example to us when we cannot control situations we care about.

REFLECTION

In what areas might we be tempted to balance biblical truth with opposing ideas in pursuit of balance? Do we pray as if we believe God can truly change hearts?

DAY 25

READ Galatians 5:7–12

By now we should be used to the strength of Paul's feeling about his opponents in Galatia! Paul loved the Galatians and wanted them to realise the danger of this false teaching. A balance between both emphases might seem wise, but Paul was no fan of balancing the truth of the gospel with the error of effort-driven godliness.

Verses 11–12 give some insight into what the false teachers were saying about Paul. Not only were they saying Paul was not a real apostle, his message was incomplete, his gospel was imbalanced and he was soft on sin but they were also accusing him of being inconsistent. Apparently they claimed that Paul preached circumcision elsewhere.

Maybe they were confused about what happened in Jerusalem with Titus (see 2:1–5), or maybe they were confused about how he followed Jewish custom in other places in order to reach the Jews with the gospel (see 1 Cor. 9:19–23). Paul was willing to do anything except sin to reach different people with the gospel – he would become all things to all men that by all means he might save some!

With those under the law he became as one under it, although he wasn't under the law. And with those not under the law he joined them, but not in sin. He was not under the law, neither was he lawless. He remained under the law of Christ, always obediently following Christ. Paul did not preach circumcision; he preached Christ and him crucified. In contrast his opponents preached angrily against immorality with lots of duty thrown in, but spoke little of Christ and the grace of God.

To finish this section Paul makes it clear whether he feels compromise with the false teachers is an option – absolutely not! Verse 12 is the strongest verse in all of Paul's writings. They are so keen on the knife, he wishes they would be bolder with it! It's harsh stuff, but so clear ... compromise with error is never the way to healthy teaching for believers, nor the path to effective evangelism among the lost. Like Paul, **we need to consistently follow Christ and proclaim Christ so that the gospel of Christ is as clear as possible for all.**

REFLECTION

How do we live among people not under the law? How do we keep from either reverting to a law lifestyle (and therefore distancing ourselves from them), or becoming lawless ourselves (and therefore undermining our message)?

DAY 26

READ Galatians 5:13–15

Paul has been clear, but there is a common misunderstanding to clear up. In Christ we are free from the law. However, is Paul suggesting that we are free to sin? He'd be shocked at the thought. We are free, yet not for our flesh to indulge itself but for us to serve others (v. 13).

Making negative statements about the law is not the same as being soft on sin. While there are many who do seem to be soft on sin, this problem will not be resolved simply by emphasising the law. Consider Paul: was he soft on sin? Absolutely not! Paul urges the Galatians not to use their freedom to indulge the flesh – their pre-programmed and biased bodies with all their impulses, rebellious tendencies and old ways of living out independence from God. Doesn't it reveal something of the power of the flesh that we automatically think the alternative to law-keeping is sin? Paul urges them, instead, to use their freedom to serve one another in love.

Maybe Paul dreamt about the impact a church marked by self-giving love would have on those around. Perhaps he imagined the impact of a church transformed by the gospel and by Christ's grace as the Spirit drew each one deeper into an intimate relationship with their Abba.

A legalistic approach to Christianity will never have that kind of impact on a community. Observers of such societies will tend to see self-righteous, pompous, aggressive and negative people who are critical, judgmental and often sadly unloving. Law never generates love; God does. Thus Paul calls for them to love their neighbour as themselves (v. 14). Love fulfils the law, so there is no need to focus on the law (see also Rom. 13:8–10).

In verse 15 Paul offers the contrast. If the Galatians choose the law-heavy version of Christianity, how will things turn out? The self-focused spirituality that comes through a law emphasis does not produce love. It turns individuals into competitors. They will bite and devour each other. There will be explosive anger, inconsistent interactions, behind-the-scenes backbiting and destructive talk. An inadequate view of the gospel will undermine the attractiveness of any community of believers.

Christ has set us free, not giving us a licence to sin, but so that we can lovingly serve.

REFLECTION

Have you experienced the difference between a Christ-focused and loving Christianity, and a self-focused and competitive Christianity? Which do you find attractive?

DAY 27

READ Galatians 5:16–18

The Christian life feels like a battle. It is. It is a continual conflict between the Spirit of God and our flesh. The Spirit wants to draw our hearts to Christ so that our lives will be transformed into Christlikeness from the inside out. Our flesh (sinful nature) is our leftover operating system from our spiritually dead days that wants to keep our hearts self-absorbed. As a Christian I can delight in Christ, while at the same time still defaulting to the idea that the pivot and fulcrum of the universe is me. That is the tension we experience in the Christian life.

The Spirit does not augment our independent efforts at righteous living, like some sort of God-given battery pack. He comes to change the way we live. We used to live one way. We are now going to live another way (v. 16).

Notice where the tension actually exists according to this passage: in our desires (vv. 16–17). It is critical that we understand the significance of the desires of the flesh and desires of the Spirit. The heart of the human problem is the human heart. The engine driving us is our 'wants', and our problem before salvation was that we only wanted what seemed best for the kingdom of self. What could change that set of 'wants'? Only the Spirit, who breathes new desires into us.

Thus the role of the Spirit is vital. In fact, if you don't understand the role of the Spirit, you cannot understand Galatians. Without the Spirit, we are spiritually dead – captured in the black hole of our self-loving desires. We might be rebellious and zealous for pleasures, or we might be religious and zealous for righteousness, but without the Spirit of God we are stuck in a vortex of self-love. The Spirit draws our loving gaze from self to the wonder of the Father's heart revealed through the Son. The Spirit stirs our hearts as the love of God is poured out into our hearts (Rom. 5:5), so that we become lovers of God (1 Jn. 4:19). **The Spirit brings a whole new set of desires and thereby changes the way we live**.

REFLECTION

How often do you feel the tension between loving yourself and loving Christ? Which set of desires have been winning in the last few days?

DAY 28

READ Galatians 5:16–21

When we become a follower of Jesus, the Spirit of God brings a whole new set of desires into our hearts. But the old self-focused desires are still present in our flesh (our bodies, our minds, our old ways of thinking, and so on). So Paul writes urging the Galatians to live by, to be led by, the Spirit. Otherwise their flesh would drive them into all sorts of ungodliness.

What happens if we turn from the influence of the Spirit and instead live according to the impulses and strength of our flesh? Read the list in verses 19–21 slowly. This is not just a list of what goes on 'out there' – out among the people who don't know God. This is a list describing the direction your own flesh will take you if you don't let the Spirit continually redirect your gaze to Christ so your desires are continually stirred by His beauty.

Notice that the list is like a sandwich. At the beginning and end there are gross sins that might seem extreme – inappropriate sensual behaviour, being drunk or engaging in vulgar acts. But in the middle there are some items Paul has already touched on in verse 15: discord, jealousy, fits of rage, selfish ambition and dissensions. How easily we can see a list like this and feel immune because of the extremes included. Yet Paul is not describing the evil world outside the church. He is describing the tendency of the flesh of people within the church. Fleshly living is fleshly living – even if it looks good on the outside. **Living by the flesh leads to evil behaviour!**

Look back to Galatians 3:1–3. Paul has been contrasting living the Christian life by the Spirit and by the flesh. The Galatians were trying to mature and grow by the efforts of their own flesh. So Paul pulls back the covers and shows the direction of 'flesh living' – it is ultimately completely ungodly. Even trying to live a good and godly life, apart from the Spirit, with my gaze on myself instead of Christ, will never lead to even a half-decent life. The flesh and the Spirit are in conflict with each other: which way will you live the Christian life?

REFLECTION

Have you ever tried to live a more godly life in your own strength and ended up struggling with sin more than ever? Thank God for giving His Spirit to draw us to Christ!

DAY 29 READ Galatians 5:16–18, 22–26

Even with all our scientific brilliance we cannot generate a single fruit merely by human effort: not a solitary grape. The same is true in the Christian life! How hard do you have to try to become joy-filled? Actually, to understand the 'fruit of the Spirit' we have to recognise that the clue is in the title. It is fruit, and it is from the Spirit.

The Spirit's work in a believer is to change their desires so that out of the heart flow the characteristics of Christ. Like any fruit, the growth will be gradual, and it will come from the inside out. Paul could easily have been thinking of Jesus' teaching at the start of John 15: 'I am the vine; you are the branches ... remain in me ... bear much fruit; apart from me you can do nothing' (Jn. 15:5).

The first fruit in Paul's list (vv. 22–23) is the defining characteristic of God and therefore of the Spirit-led follower of Christ: love. The love of God overflowing from our hearts toward God and others results in four pairs of beautiful Christ-like qualities:

1. Joy and peace – our lives can celebrate the goodness of God's loving rule in the midst of a chaotic world.
2. Patience (ESV) and kindness – we can genuinely react to others in a way their actions don't deserve, just like Christ.
3. Goodness and faithfulness – we can manifest a self-giving love and loyalty in reflection of Christ's character.
4. Gentleness and self-control – our lives are not stirred by fleshly self-protective aggression, but by the combination of humility, tender love and resolute holiness that characterised Christ.

Notice that Paul twice mentions law – in verse 18 and again in 23. Why? Because he wants them to realise that what is needed in the Christian life is heart change, not renewed focus on the law. The law never changes hearts. But changed hearts more than fulfil the law! Love God and love others, by the work of the Spirit in you, and your holiness will surpass what the law requires. (Paul also says this in Romans 13:8–10.) When Christ died on that cross, the old 'kingdom of self' desires were also crucified (v. 24). It is as if Paul is proclaiming, 'Welcome to the wonder of the life I now live!'

REFLECTION

How do you see the fruit of the Spirit growing in your life? In what areas might God's Spirit be nurturing your character currently?

DAY 30

READ Galatians 6:1–5

Paul wanted the Galatians to live out the gospel: not focusing on their own efforts and ending up with a fleshly, sour, competitive community, but rather focusing on Christ, walking in step with the Spirit, and ending up with a beautiful, selfless, godly community.

When a Christian sins, do they typically long to go to church, or do they instinctively withdraw from church? A church characterised by fleshly competitiveness will usually be rife with hypocrisy and criticism. Consequently a sinning believer would rather run away than run to church. But when a church is made up of people living Paul's type of Christianity, then you will find a community of authentic and loving people – they may be struggling with sin, but they are gripped by the grace of God and ready to support one another!

Sin brings with it a terrible weight. There is the guilt, the shame, the broken relationships, the numerous consequences. When we cannot be real with one another, then this burden is huge. A gospel-gripped community will help carry that burden together (v. 2). Obviously only the death of Christ can pay for the guilt, and when helping a believer caught in a sin we need to be careful lest we get caught up in it, but the community of Christ's people can reach out to lovingly restore the repentant believer (v. 1).

In verses 3–5 Paul ends up saying each person should bear his own load. Is this a contradiction? No. Paul is switching to the self-focused version of Christianity offered by the false teachers in Galatia. In their version of the faith, the focus is on myself as I measure myself against my preferred set of laws. I become competitive with others as I compare myself to them. This leads to believers putting legalistic burdens on each other, which is the opposite of a true gospel community. So Paul writes that we are each to carry our own load (the word in verse 5 is like a backpack – the life God gives us), but then look to help one another with their burden (the word in verse 2 refers to a heavy weight).

A gospel-gripped community will be self-giving, rather than self-righteous. **Instead of imposing our version of godly standards on those around us, thereby crushing others with our legalism, we will lovingly reach out to support each other**.

REFLECTION

Who can you lovingly support today?

DAY 31

READ Galatians 6:6–8

There are two versions of the Christian life. One is focused on myself and my efforts, the other is focused on Christ and His goodness. Paul continues to show that there is only one way to live the life we now have in Christ.

In verse 6 Paul addresses care for teachers. He knew that he was on the receiving end of some heavy-duty criticism among the Christians in Galatia. Just as a fleshly self-focused attempt to live the Christian life will result in a community biting and devouring one another (5:15), so also it will result in chewing up the preacher too. Too many Christians have an appetite for roast preacher!

A community marked by the fruit of the Spirit will be a community that cares for one another. This includes care for those who preach the Bible to them, through sharing encouragement and financial support. True believers will not be consumers who simply take from a church; they will be participants who share in the giving.

In verses 7–8 Paul shares his underlying principle throughout the application section of the letter. Believers can either invest their energy in their own flesh, or in the Spirit. Instead of using the language to 'walk by the Spirit ... keep in step with the Spirit' (5:16 ESV, 25,), he now uses the farming language of sowing and reaping. If believers sow their lives in flesh living, then they will harvest a crop that is consistent with that – a crop of corruption. If believers sow their lives to the Spirit, then there will be an eternally wonderful crop.

What does it mean to 'sow to please the Spirit?' In light of all that we have seen, this must mean the opposite of living according to the flesh. It is living with my focus not on myself, but on Christ; not living with a focus on my performance, but on his goodness; a life defined not by my independence, but by my absolute dependence. This life is not about self-gratifying pleasure-seeking, nor self-righteous religiosity, but Christ-loving relationship.

God cannot be mocked – we will reap what we sow. God has given us a new way to live, but if we resist that offer and live by our own fleshly independence, then eventually the corruption will be evident to all!

REFLECTION

As you ponder the way you are investing your life's energies today, what will you be reaping in the future?

DAY 32

READ Galatians 5:16, 18, 25; 6:8

Let's think some more about what it means to live by the Spirit, to be led by the Spirit, to sow to please the Spirit.

If we are to sow to please the Spirit, what pleases the Spirit? If we were to read through the whole New Testament and look for teaching about the Holy Spirit, we would get a clear sense of what pleases the Spirit:

- The Spirit cares about the oneness of the Father and the Son – the relationship of the God who is Trinity.
- He cares about our relationship with God. It's the Spirit that sealed us. It's the Spirit that pours out the love of God into our hearts. It's the Spirit that takes our prayers and brings them to the Father. It's the Spirit that cares about us understanding the Word that He inspired. The Spirit is passionate about communication – God to us and us to God.
- He cares about our relationships with each other. He cares about how we use His gifts to build one another up in the body of Christ. He wants our words to give grace to each other, and when they don't He is grieved.

So what does it mean to sow to the Spirit? At the very least, it must mean the following:

- It means having a heart that is open to God's word. We will spend time in the Bible, getting to know God more, allowing His Spirit to shape and change what we love, how we think, and how we live.
- It means praying to God with a transparent vulnerability. Instead of perfunctory prayers spoken without an engaged heart, or selfish prayers offered in a demanding tone, we will pray and lay our hearts bare before God, seeking His desire in each situation that concerns us or Him.
- It means caring about our relationships with each other in the church. We will pursue honesty, graciousness, and building others up. The Spirit is pleased when we care for each other, express appreciation, and stop gossip in its tracks.

If we will sow to the Spirit then we will reap the harvest of a church community that is truly delightful.

REFLECTION

Consider your local church community. Praise God for every aspect that is delightfully Christ-like. Pray for God to lead your church toward a harvest of delightful Christ-likeness. Ask that He begin in you.

READ Galatians 6:9–10

At the end of his life and ministry, Moses gave the people two alternatives. They could be faithful to God or faithless (Deut. 30:15–20). At the end of his life and ministry, Joshua did the same – see Joshua 24:14–15. Now Paul wraps up Galatians with a similar call. The Galatians could accept God's glorious provision in Christ, by the Spirit, or they could reject that and live life based on the desires of their own flesh. **Living in light of the gospel will be worth it in the end**.

The principle Paul gave in verses 7–8 was simple: we always reap according to what we sow. Put in carrot seed and you will eventually be pulling out carrots. Sow to the flesh and the result will be corruption. Or sow to the Spirit and the result will be life.

We should heed Paul's warning in this simple principle. Perhaps you are sowing to the flesh? Maybe there is an ongoing secret sin that is consuming your energy and resources? And perhaps God doesn't seem to be disciplining or rescuing you? Maybe you are getting away with it and nobody is getting hurt? God cannot be mocked. Respond to this warning because you will not be the exception. Sowing to the flesh will reap destruction in your relationships, in your family, in your church. Trust God's word and turn to Him now.

Maybe you are doing respectable Christianity in your own strength? Perhaps you are keeping up appearances without any meaningful connection to God? Maintaining this mask will also lead to a negative harvest in your life, and in your church.

However, we should also hear the encouragement in this simple principle. Don't give up doing good (v. 9)! Perhaps you are giving yourself away in serving others, caring for children, teaching a Sunday-school class, looking after a difficult relative, caring pastorally for difficult people in the church – don't give up! It may seem fruitless right now. It may feel like every drop of love you give instantly disappears without recognition, like water into parched soil, but don't give up. There will be a harvest.

Paul wants gospel-gripped believers to give of themselves just like God has given of Himself – with no immediate reward, but with an unending eternal harvest to come.

REFLECTION

Where are you tempted to give up doing good? How can you encourage someone else to not give up doing good?

DAY 34

READ Galatians 6:11–13

As Paul wraps up the powerful letter to the Galatians, he makes a reference to his handwriting (v. 11). Presumably he had been dictating the letter to this point, but he wants them to be certain the letter has come from him. So he writes a line himself and knows they will recognise his larger script. He will do anything to make sure they hear the message of this letter.

Then in verses 12–13 he returns to the false teachers, to shine a light on their motives. They sounded so pious encouraging the Galatians to come under the burden of circumcision and law-keeping. But what was their real motive? They were not seeking to benefit the Galatian believers, but rather to bolster their own reputation. They wanted to have a badge of honour to protect themselves from any persecution associated with the radical message of the cross.

So often there is a profound inconsistency in people preaching passionately for certain kinds of behaviour. They seem so committed to a certain lifestyle, but their own private reality does not live up to their words. Like a strong-looking log that is riddled with rot, they lack the integrity everyone assumes they have.

Paul is so strongly opposed to false teachers. **We must not be naïve: false teachers still exist today**. They present a passionate plea for holiness, but do so for their own benefit. True gospel preachers preach Christ and the fruit is a greater and a more genuine holiness.

The false teachers opposing Paul sounded so Christian. Yet false teachers add something to the gospel of God's grace. They turn the focus from Christ to self. They make a lot of noise about holiness, but the wonder of Christ and His work tends to fade from centre stage. They are in it for themselves.

Martin Luther wrote,

But the holier the heretics seem to be in external appearance, the more damage they cause. For if the false apostles had not possessed outstanding gifts, great authority, and the appearance of holiness; and if they had not claimed to be ministers of Christ, pupils of the apostles, and sincere preachers of the gospel, they could not so easily have undermined the authority of Paul and made an impression on the Galatians.[4]

REFLECTION

Pray for the Bible teachers in your church. Ask God to continue to woo their hearts to Christ and keep them true to Him.

DAY 35

READ Galatians 6:14–17

In human terms, Paul had every reason to boast. He had preached the gospel in Galatia. He had seen people getting saved. He had seen churches started. But that is not why he boasts. His only boast is in the cross of Jesus Christ (v. 14a)!

Here are two great truths in summary at the end of the letter:

1. Paul's fleshly life, as far as he is concerned, was crucified with Christ (v. 14b). Paul called himself the chief of sinners, but that sin was not simply murder and terrorism. It was *religious* terrorism! If you look in Philippians 3:4–6, Paul lists all the religious things he could take pride in before, but not now. He goes on to write there that fleshly religiousness is dung compared to knowing Christ.
2. As well as boasting in Christ crucified, Paul is also refusing to let religious codes dictate distinctions. Neither circumcision nor uncircumcision matter now (v. 15). It is not about Jewishness or Gentileness. It is not about being a law-keeper. The only thing that counts now is a 'new creation'. What is this referring to? In 2 Corinthians 5:17 Paul uses the same language to speak of those who are in Christ – they are a 'new creation' – and that is at the conclusion of a wonderful section all about the New Covenant. **Because of Christ's death at Calvary, the Spirit comes to bring us into fellowship with God, our Abba, transforming us from the inside out.**

In verse 16 Paul wants to bless everyone who agrees with his gospel – not only Gentile believers who celebrate the no-circumcision gospel, but also, and especially, the believers with a Jewish background who also grasp Paul's teaching. These people knew that being circumcised is not a problem; it is just not the issue.

In verse 17 Paul returns to the subject of carrying burdens. He refers to the marks he bears or carries on his own body. He has suffered for this glorious gospel for which he is so passionate. If he had been in Galatia he might have simply taken off his shirt and shown his own back – covered in scars, many of which had come from very religious opponents, because proclaiming the gospel of God's grace in Christ is worth suffering for!

REFLECTION

How passionate are you for the simple gospel of God's glorious grace? Ask God for clarity (what is the gospel?) and courage (will I stand for it?).

DAY 36

READ Galatians 2:20 – 3:3 and 6:18

Nobody was born a Christian. We were born dead in sin and 'lived' a fleshly life: an independent 'I can do it on my own, God!' kind of life. Some have a fleshly appetite for licentious pleasures. Others have a fleshly appetite for respect from the religious community. Either way, this independent living is not really living at all. It is spiritually dead.

At some point, if you are a Christian, God got a hold of your life. By His Spirit He drew your gaze to Christ on the cross. He poured out His love into you, and He did something inside of you. This is the transformation Paul passionately defended: the New Covenant. Yet this new heart, with new desires and the Spirit dwelling within, is all dwelling within our flesh – which is why we are all conflicted people. We long to please God, but our flesh always turns back, trying to live independently from God.

Paul did not want the Galatians to lose the gospel by merely adding in a self-focused ingredient of performance. There must be no turning from the New Covenant back to a perversion of the Old Covenant, either for salvation or for growth in godliness. Why turn from Christ to yourself? Why stop living by the Spirit and start living by your own effort? The law was never designed to create righteousness. It was designed to expose your unrighteousness. The law was given to show that you were dead in your sins and you need God to do something in you. Why would you turn your back on God and go after a religious approach to life that is all about yourself?

Even in the last verse (v. 18), Paul reiterates his point. It is about grace, not law. It is the Lord Jesus Christ, not me. It is His work within us (in our spirit by His Spirit – His grace), not our work.

If we let Galatians grip us, then we will be passionate about Christ and the cross. We will be stirred by the Spirit inside us, drawing us closer to our Abba. And the fruit will be a holy community of believers driven not by dutiful determination, but by delight in our fellowship with the Trinity. We will not be self-focused but others-focused. **The gospel changes everything: it gives us a whole new kind of life to live!**

REFLECTION

Thank God for the life He has for you!

REFERENCES

1 *Luther's Works,* vol. 26: Lectures on Galatians, 1535, Chapters 1-4 (Missouri: Concordia, 1963), p. 26.

2 *Luther's Works*, vol. 26, pp. 63-64.

3 *Luther's Works*, vol. 26, p. 54.

4 *Luther's Works*, vol. 26, p. 52.

MORE IN THIS SERIES

ROMANS
Momentous News
By David Cook
ISBN: 978-1-906173-24-1

MARK
The Suffering Servant
By Jeremy McQuoid
ISBN: 978-1-906173-55-5

DANIEL
Far From Home
By Justin Mote
ISBN: 978-1-906173-68-5

1 THESSALONIANS
Living for Jesus
By Julia Marsden
ISBN: 978-1-906173-67-8

PHILIPPIANS
Press towards the Goal
By Kay Mumford
ISBN: 978-1-909611-31-3

ESTHER
Silent but Sovereign
By Carolyn Lacey
ISBN: 978-1-909611-84-9

ACTS
To the Ends of the Earth
By David Cook
ISBN: 978-1-909611-02-3

EZEKIEL
For His Glory
By Peter Lau
ISBN: 978-1-909611-83-2

JOHN
Never Thirst Again
By David Cook
ISBN: 978-1-909611-30-6

Peter Mead
GALATIANS
36 UNDATED DEVOTIONS THROUGH THE BOOK OF GALATIANS